THE EGG OF ZERO

Philip Gross was born in 1952 in Delabole, Cornwall, grew up in Plymouth, and now lives with his wife Zélie in Bristol, teaching Creative Writing at the University of Glamorgan. He has worked with every step on the educational ladder from nursery to PhD, is a Quaker and a horror writer, balances his poetry and fiction with work for radio, the occasional stage play and children's opera, and enjoys collaboration with musicians, painters, dancers and writers of all kinds.

Since winning a Gregory Award in 1981 and first prize in the National Poetry Competition in 1982 he has published books with Peterloo, Faber and Bloodaxe, including *The Air Mines of Mistila*, with Sylvia Kantaris (1988: Poetry Book Society Choice) and *The Wasting Game* (1998: shortlisted for the Whitbread Poetry Award). Poems from all these and several small-press collections are brought together in *Changes of Address: Poems 1980-1998* (Bloodaxe Books, 2001). His latest collections are *Mappa Mundi* (Bloodaxe Books, 2003), a Poetry Book Society Recommendation, and *The Egg of Zero* (Bloodaxe Books, 2006).

His poetry for children includes *Manifold Manor*, *The All-Nite Café* (winner of the Signal Award 1994) and *Scratch City*, all from Faber, who also published his first novel for young people, *The Song of Gail and Fludd*, in 1991. Since then Scholastic have published five more; his first for Oxford University Press was *Going For Stone* (2002), described by *The Guardian* as 'wonderfully scary and unusual'.

PHILIP GROSS

THE Egg OF Zero

BLOODAXE BOOKS

ISBN: 1 85224 726 6

First published 2006 by
Bloodaxe Books Ltd,
Highgreen,
Tarset,
Northumberland NE48 1RP.

www.bloodaxebooks.com
For further information about Bloodaxe titles
please visit our website or write to
the above address for a catalogue.

Bloodaxe Books Ltd acknowledges
the financial assistance of
Arts Council England, North East.

Cover printing by J. Thomson Colour Printers Ltd, Glasgow.

Printed in Great Britain by
Bell & Bain Limited, Glasgow.

Once and for all –
to save dedicating every other poem in this book:

To Zélie

ACKNOWLEDGEMENTS

Acknowledgements are due to the editors of the following publications in which some of these poems first appeared: *Agenda, Amsterdam Review, City: Bristol in Poems* (Paralalia, 2004), *Leviathan Quarterly, London Magazine, Magma, New Welsh Review, Poetry, Poetry London, Poetry Review, Poetry Wales, Rattapallax, The North, The Reader, The Rialto* and *Vallum*.

Particular thanks are due to Nicolas McDowall of the Old Stile Press for encouragement and publication, as *The Abstract Garden* (2006), of my collaboration with engraver Peter Reddick which was the genesis of several poems in this book.

Also to Evie Wyld for a line in 'Survivors', to Bridget Thomas for some choice words in 'The Old Order', to Judy Kendall for the Japanese in 'Translated', and to Jeremy and Mario for their incisive, often opposite, advice.

CONTENTS

Having Built the Pleasure Dome

And now it's done
    unmake it,
        ripping screens and furnishings away.

(Almost too much
    to consider the hand-
        and eye-work that went in

to all this lumber.)
    Leave the walls and door-
        and window-sockets bare

for what light will,
    for the small rains and sparrows,
        and there, dead centre on the floor

(you can't get round it)
    leave the stone, one plain
        unwrought jack-naked block (no

labels, not a word
    of explanation) like a tiny mountain
        that shrinks all the building round it

to perspective, or an empty chest
    turned deftly inside out, so all
        the world that stood around it looking in

is *inside*, and out here,
    the space it held. *Stet.* Leave
        the stone. And night and morning,

night and morning turn
    to face it. Presence. What
        it might be. What it might be *for*.

Fire Forms

1

My father had a way with fire:
the candle-flame cupped in his hands

as if he'd given birth to it.

It was a man thing, this
familiarity. My mother winced away.

He tamed it with a slow stroke

of his finger through the flame
which did him no harm; no, it curled

to his touch; it rubbed itself against him

till he licked his thumb and finger tip
and pinched its life out, gently, at the root.

This gift could be mine too, like a son's

right... I just had to be sure –
hesitate, and you're burned.

It looked like a chance not worth taking

and I didn't...until thirty years later
with my son's eyes watching me.

And it did hurt, and I didn't say.

2

They met one night
in the Fire Garden.
Found the gate
unpadlocked, leading
off no particular street

where no such gate had been.
It might have been lit
for them alone:
small flames in a tight
unwavering line

like crocus buds, mauve-blue
or yellow. (Bunsen
burners, he thought, in a school
lab.) Further on,
a low pale

flickering, scarcely warm
like flambéed alcohol,
enticed them from
the path. They bent to smell
the off-sweet perfume

of the creeping *feu
d'artifice*, spark weed
that grew everywhere
you didn't look. At their feet
spreading fissures

in the pavement leaked
a moss of clinker-
glow, like a peat
bog burning for years
underground. All that night

they were only the glow
of their skins. Come morning,
they were their own
shadows walking,
matt and apart. Hold a spoon

to a candle: your reflection
is a molten drip, then
soot. Stealth coating:
no blip on the radar screen
of you. Pure carbon.

3

It's not we who undo you; you
give way, break down, release your grip

on your molecules. We tread as light as we can

as your firewalkers do upon us, not
quite touching. We are your companions

through the furnace in our sheaths of light,

our loose-furled desert robes:
angeloi, messengers, with no message

except what we are – a translation

of you, into our tongues, celebration
even now, as you lie down

in yourselves, your bed

of cinders. Through, by and on we pass
tactfully, leaving no print in your ash.

Translucence

A drip of wax, spilled on the white
spread linen: there's a mystery
I dwelt on while the grown-ups talked.
Lift it up, just enough: an under-light

inhered in what was stain, and shade
in the white around it – *via negativa*
for beginners in a tear-splash spot
that was almost a spy hole, contact made

with a close world unknown as next door.
The wax was, somehow, soft *and* brittle:
it rucked, then crinkled to the touch,
like silk decayed, the wedding dress I saw

in its museum case (How small had she been,
the dead bride?) so the light inside
the fabric was a body, immaterial,
that filled it, like the chamber of the queen

of a smoked-out beehive: wing-dust, honey-rot.
Out of the strong came forth sweetness,
said the Tate & Lyle tin, with a lion
stretched out, maybe sleeping, maybe not.

Great Western

(for Peter Redgrove, 1932-2003)

Trundling under the girders of the grey bowed
boiler-plated bridge into Cornwall, I see you

as Brunel in the guise of a country parson, captain
of the industrial-scale forging of the soul,

drawn up to your full height overhung by huge
cogs and chains, the humming manufactory,

the clank of trucks, their couplings, shunting matter in
raw, to be shipped out as wonder... To where

is immaterial; the truth is in the thud and flare,
the muscles of steam flexing into the atmosphere –

call it a vast updraught of hot air
but look: anvils, thunderheads...and feel the rain,

unexpectedly gentle and generous – the Cornish
weather, Peter, never quite the same again.

Every Last Thing

(Oxford-Duden Pictorial Dictionary)

The man, the woman, in a world of nouns:
page 42: *The Living Room.*
Her mouth is open, his face turned...
    They have no verb but *be.*

Around them in the air like bugs
or angels, numbers silently alight
on things: *Table. Chair.* Outside
    the margins is a litany –

Encyclopaedia (in several volumes).
Globe. Brass kettle. Telescope.
Pipe rack. Bust – like a chant in a cave
    by monks who never see

the world but tell it over, keeping all
in being; if one of them stumbles
some which or what falls silent, un-
    knowable, a mystery

in somebody's hands. (You know
the feeling.) Every last thing, from
Hydrogen atom (p.1) to (p.384)
    Capsule, containing seeds,

from *Aaron's Rod* and *Abacus* to *Zoom-*
stereomicroscope and *Zulu.* We could build
a coking plant (p.156) or have a stab
    (p.19) at a tracheotomy

or say These are our lives (p.42):
man, woman, in our calm cartoon,
    two glasses raised to thoughts made out
    of missing pronouns – *I, you, we...*

We could set a whole new creature down
on a bare world with this manual
    in its hand, and it could recreate
    all our mistakes, eventually.

Well May You Ask

(14 everyday koans)

Do you do it on purpose, the hairs in the bath, crumbs and smears
in the butter, do you lie awake planning the next day's irritations,
just for me? / Was there nothing in his behaviour all those years
that gave cause for concern? / Doctor, say something. Doctor?
/ You boy. Yes, you! What's the meaning of this? / Why
won't anyone believe me when I tell them that I lied? /
How sad is that – I mean, to the nearest fluid ounce of tears? /
Oh, how long will the continents labour before they give birth? /
Under the fingernails, don't beat about the bush, man, are there
any *signs*? / What could have possessed us? / What time of night
do you call this? / What the hell, in heaven's name, on earth...? /
Don't you see: everything was *meant*? / Or was the whole circus
a diversion from another drama played just out of sight? / *Enough*?
Is it ever enough? God, do I have to spell it out for you?

koan: in Zen Buddhist practice, a question for meditation, to which
no logical answer is possible.

16

The Assembled

1

Chin up, the way you'd hope
    to face a firing squad,
on the school field annually

six hundred boys were racked
    by size, the smallest barecrosslegged,
seniors up on benches at the back.

Hold it... Hold... A mechanical
    whirring panned the rank.
Long tradition perfected the arc,

so that we came out straight,
    in a yard-wide photo, our faces too
perfectly straight, old boys already,

in front of the limestone façade
    (*Colonnade*, we had to say, as if
in the Latin, as if we were Classical,

above the smells of ripe creek mud,
    the Courage brewery, the lasting tang
of the military wards these blocks had been

with sergeant-matrons, bath-chairs
    for the officers, the other ranks
on crutches, tarred stumps)

the façade...which bulged into queasy
    perspective both ways, as if at one
end you might glimpse Florence Nightingale

– at the other, all our lives to come.

2

Friends... Quite what the word meant then
    escapes me. We had them:
    names our parents would learn
to ask after, and might never meet.

Did we talk? About what? We had so little
    history in us – the one
    family each, which was the only
one, ever, in the world, so what's to say?

In place of life stories, we had hobbies,
    sticking in, making lists
    and saving things so insignificant
I can't remember what mine were – only,

somewhere in the process, was the bleak
    exhilaration of having
    got, at last, the *whole set of...*
what? Who cared? It was something to be.

3

Strangers in blazers... How could we have not
demanded to know who we were? A few

of us might learn, like girls, the hard hurt-politics
of making/breaking friends but basically – boys –

we were solid, we were bricks, we were the wall
we might never see over. We had characters,

one feature each; we were caricatures
(quite animated, being children after all).

No first names: that established,
masters gifted us with nicknames

from *their* schooldays, which we never
understood. I see us in ranks,

in uniform, in Assembly, in that long
shot on the school field, our expressions

rusting into monochrome. I see us
like a shield wall – Spartans at the pass –

our orders: *Hold it... Hold...* I see us
buried, terracotta warriors in a tomb.

Big Snow,

        the first of the winter, and
people leapt in their cars to meet it,
forging up the moor side till they hit
irrefutable drifts, slewing off at lax angles
anywhere, a festival of rules suspended,

as families came tumbling out, into
the bear hug of whiteness, in their bright
snow clobber – puce, plum, vermilion
swaddlings, mittens, hoods and puffy boots –
and everyone as pudgy-limbed as toddlers

stumbling off into the stuff at random
gladly, staggered by the revelatory
new land forms – like a high surf
crashing round them that's their friend –
stumbling off but slower now, and now

at a standstill ten yards from the car,
with laughter that was half their body's
fear as the cold struck them speechless,
breath-forsaken, the way it had stroked
every boulder and bush into white-water

stasis such as you'd glimpse in the moment
you drowned – such egregious cold
they trusted it, perversely, like a brawny
uncle back from years "abroad", where
who knows what he does or might have done.

Day One

One day the plans
took leave of their drawing-boards. Tangents
went off wildly; graphs extrapolated
where they'd never dared.
It was the great escape
from two dimensions. Some lines came spiralling out
towards us; others plunged in and away, as though
inventing depth. The shift
was a red one in places,
in others, blue – the spectrum was in two minds –
and between, in the cracks, came earth tones,
ochre, umber, verdigris –
beneath the fingernails
of things…and with them texture grew, or was it
decomposing into life, as if on the eighth day
God said *Let it age. Now*
let there be decay.
and there was the richness of the grainy
and the gritty, mulch, the slippy, the ribby,
the snagged, the threadbare.
He saw it was good.
He'd still left the absolutes, out somewhere
in the not-too-interfering distance, like the blue
horizon seas did by themselves.
But here,
now, this one day, the studio wrecked itself –
the Big Bang – and the simple nomads
of the picture plane
spilled out into the world.
We followed them through, you and I, breathless,
knowing – our Day One – there was no going back
to the flat earth again.

Plymouth Hoe, with Aunt G.

(for GMH, 1924-2003)

As if for you, the Sound stages
    a weather display: a wedge of storm
    like a ploughshare, a bench plane,
        works along the horizon, behind
        the breakwater, underlined by it.
        Between the cloud-ceiling and sea

is a low cramped room
    with pink flickers of lightning,
    faulty neon. Our wound-up windows
        whine as a gust veers this way.
        We sit tight. There's another,
        a squall-dance fifty yards offshore,

the water creamed to stiff peaks.
    The breakwater fort goes filmy,
    a Victorian engraving of itself
        beneath protective paper. There's
        a dogfish frigate, overtaken
        by a moving line of...not light

but a duller glittering, a silver-nitrate
    quality to the air above, the sea
    beneath it: a motionless rufflement,
        coming, head-on, personal.
        (This outing is your last, though I
        don't know that. You might.) Then

it doesn't reach us, no, it smokes off
    sideways, quite a different story,
    and here's brightness crystallising out
        into rickety cloud-heaps
        with a stunned new blue behind them
        and the sun not here, not yet,

but ready for an entrance
like a clash of cymbals. So why
not rejoice, why not believe
we've been invited, called as witnesses,
to fix the moment, its and ours,
before the whole show blows away?

Thin Houses

Whether a cracked refraction in the train's
scratched glass, or Inter-City speed,
foreshortened something for me, still, I saw
what I saw: a cake-slice of thirty degrees

of brick between the railway and the street,
which made a sharp house, not a room thick,
barely more than a stage flat or the façade
of a dolls' house you unhook and hinge back

on furniture stood in a line as if affronted.
(All the door-framed perspectives enticing you in
to pry are *trompe l'oeil*, near, and painted.)
A thin house...like our first together, narrowing

to a prow: one desk, one window. The bridge
of a ship. The downside of the city was the swell
the road plunged into. Russian Vine swamped the wedge
of a garden, white and green like foam, as one hill

rolled towards us, one heaved up behind. Seasick
sometimes with the sense of what we'd done,
leaving possessions, *possession*, flotsammed in our wake,
I recalled, from some boys' annual, we had to hold on

and steer straight at it. Our pasts were on board,
and our future, and the consequences – part crew,
part stowaways. Only inches of the pinkwashed walls
kept the whole of our lives from being on view

to the world – a provisional house between converging
streets, between closing-time brawls, between Irish, Urdu,
Jamaican, dub bass and the weep of trucks at dawn reversing.
We breathed in. We grew a little thinner. We came through.

The City Between

Between states of light – *entre chien*
et loup – someone clatters a pan
    through a barred courtyard window.

The donkey they threw down the well
in the Hundred Years War is still
    braying, bricked-in, in the first van's

or the last's sound, loading. And a gull
starts up, and up, as if just recalling
    the sea, was it, that left the harbour

years ago? *Entre chien et loup*
don't ask the people passing, few
    and heads down, if they're stragglers

from a day's work or creeping awake.
And the light on that gull like an ash-flake
    from the burning might be dusk

or dawn, don't ask, for down among
the greyish dogs, the not-bad hang-
    dog dogs, is where I come,

        dear *loup*, to meet you.

Mnemonic

As the old orators paced out their logic
on a map of Rome, inside them
     like The Knowledge, so

the squints and ginnels of our city,
the parallel streets that sometimes
     meet, the junctions that don't,

the clutter shops where you might find,
say, a knife-sharpener's wheel
     beside a crimping iron

and a bamboo tricycle so fine
that only a raffia-boned child
     could ride it, stalls

where women shrivelled to essentials
bring their folding-tables-full
     of chanterelles, boletus,

things you have to take their word
for and a jar of bright berries
     they stroke out like beads,

all these – and the bomb site's
feral kittens, and the four lane
     traffic loosed

from the lights like boulders
in a flash flood – are the shape,
     in real, in stone

and stucco, in street cries,
in there-and-gone shop-doorway
     smells like *déjà vu*

out of no childhoods we ever had –
the shape of how we looked,
               talked and walked it all

into ourselves, the way they took
to heart their own, their city,
               those old Romans,

and the logic followed, necessarily.

Tallinn, 2004

The Age We Are

A world at our feet: it opens, down into the maw
of the mall – we two on one step of the escalator.
    Already we're part, not foreign
bodies, of its body, half digested by the age we are.

The rate of circulation, that's what counts. Why else
would the revolving doors, and the muzac, go
    just so, in sync? If unaccountably
somebody stopped – worse, *sat*...then they'd see

they'd been seen: condensing out of an air
of vague vigilance, personnel in tactful uniforms,
    the pastel police, would be there
in the crowd, one either side, to shift them.

*

Late capitalism, wasn't that what we said
    in the New Left,
best part of a lifetime ago? Something
    is late, all right, but
what, we won't know, until...later.

*

Out of all corners of the eye
I keep catching us, out-of-bodied, grey,
from above and behind
on CCTV. And mirrors,
mirrors: we're never alone.
Always crowds of ourselves.

Sometimes we're children
taken shopping, plodding
through continual Christmas.
Other times I surprise us,

when we think nobody's looking
(I am that nobody, looking),

fifty-something, holding hands...

*

Crystal Palaces? They're two a penny now –
one on everybody's outskirts, bright, so bright

and see-through as the dark falls. Asking for it,
so much glass. One pulse, a shudder: it could rise

and spread wings into splinters round us,
like a flock of startled knives.

*

It doesn't cost, I tell myself, just looking – gawping
                with the kind of awe
a Dacian legionary might have felt in Rome on furlough.

Or is this the latest pastime in the Land of Late,
                in any *ancien régime*:
to fancy yourself the barbarian – Marie Antoinette

in her toy cottage playing shepherdesses? (What
                do you mean: *sheep*?)

*

The wonder of it is
– there is
a wonder in it –
how it came to be

just like that.
Round the margins
of thousand-space parking lots
ragwort and thistles

29

nod and wag
like bumpkins. *Did you
see where that
came from? Damned*

if I did. A quick-
fruiting cash crop
in between the airfield
and the M4/M5 interchange,

between the profit margin
and the cost of petrol. That's
a kind of wonder, too:
tireless and watchful

as guardian angels,
the data.
The plotted co-ordinates
that say: *Here,*

now. That say:
*You know it's what
you wanted.*
And it seems to be.

*

Does it hurt? No, it's more
of an itch, a kind of rumble

when it can't be time to eat yet.
All snacks between meals.

Something hurts for the child
strapped in like a test pilot

in his padded buggy, throwing
his arms and legs out suddenly –

eject! Or the fourteen year old
who can't look away though she's sick

to the stomach with the plaster model's
midriff. Or the stand-offs round that one

somehow perfect parking bay. No, that's
not *hurting*, is it? More the dull place

like scar tissue, where there's no
sensation but I have to scratch it,

like this. Scratch it till (a sign
of life) it starts to bleed.

*

To find ourselves here
at this juncture, at this hour
near closing, or at all,

in not the first flush,
in the fullness of
ourselves, in awe

among the play of lights
across dark water, here
the floating world

in which we've found
each other, here the garden
of ripe appetites...

*

And somehow even this turns out to be a love song
        as the steel stairs take us down: we're here
           a little damaged but still standing,
                dropped over the edge

into the deep end of a century that we'd never
        imagined, not seriously (as children will
           be serious) we'd see. Recall
                those children now,

31

play-barbarians in from the wastes of the fields
at the back of the school, from dens
on bombsites. Call them
in. 'The 50s' –

'Post-war' – don't the words sound comforting
and dull, like shutters being rattled up
on the newly-reopened shop
of Ordinary. Pudging

noses on the glass, those children, staring in
now at this bright world...Pointing
at us, something like them-
selves, transfigured,

grey-haired. But (as
if it's never too late) advancing
down the glowing vista, Startrite-fashion.
And into the gingerbread house, holding hands.

A Chance of Dragons

Station Road, Chinese New Year

The dragon stamps, it stamps and flares
in a *cul-de-sac* backstreet, with viaduct walls
in smokestone, falls of ivy
                              – a place with an air
of being cobbled though it's not, somewhere
a van could park until its tyres go down,

between the faces beaming from their billboard
on the corner (five times our size, five times sleeker
like gods of impossible fortune)
                              and the winos' secret
trash-and-mattress cave. Outside a square and low
brick warehouse, on a ramp of forklift pallets, there

the year begins; it comes out bright and papery
as painted fire, a dragon that could fold into a largish
suitcase in a cargo hold.
                              Here it comes, out of sour-
sweet-and-musty emporium smells, from a world
that opens inwards implausibly far, to candies,

movie mags and cleavers, diligence and abalone shells,
dried duck with beak and feet on (but flattened,
with a tarry look like roadkill),
                              cut price flights
to Hong Kong (two way), lanterns, sacks
of bean sprouts big as bolsters, and a shrine.

Here it comes, with half a man still visible
inside, part swallowed, half of him its legs that stamp
out the swagger and ripple and sway,
                              for us all,
the idlest passers-by, the most hurrying-home
wherever home may be, however far.

And now the train wheels spark and thump
on the viaduct: firecrackers, promising
the chance of dragons
                    anywhere.

Sailors

The child next door is crying (the wind
is too big and too sudden, and it's 4 A.M.,
the wind is out of place, it's bullying the windows)
                    – crying loud enough

I can't ignore it through the gusts,
as it drops to a dull whine when the wind does
then, like it, rallies to round on itself.
                    His father's voice,

now it comes, comes in gradually abrading
measured lengths, but you might as well try
to reach an understanding with the wind
                    as it stumbles on into us,

into the land, into this house or that
and nobody can hold it... stumbles on
with the other winds crowding in behind,
                    through all the world

in which they have no habitation. There's an edge
of cracking in the man's voice like faulty reception, what
more can he say, he's said it calmly twice, he won't say it again...
                    Pity the sailors

on a night like this, my Cornish grandmother
said, without fail, and I knew what she meant
(though I don't think she knew any sailors,
                    and neither did I).

Rock Stump in the Desert

Turned on a lathe
of blown sand
(tiny silica blades
at their sharpest a foot from the ground)

it's stone's joke
of golfball on its tee
that one whack of a storm
could send spinning. It gives you thoughts

like these: the ambulating
rocks of the Mojave's
salt-pan flats
on which a boulder leaves its slower-

than-a-snail-trail track,
a little wavering, as if
there was a mind there
to be not quite made up. You could want

to take it home with you
in the back of the pickup,
give it free range in the garden.
You could fool yourself you might be friends,

that it might whisper
to you, with its faint
dry keening, all it knows
of desert, of no you, of world without end.

Red Kites Rising

Ease
has nothing to do with it. The wind machine
is cranking. It's a Puffing Billy of a day.

High-sided vehicles quail, think better
and shift down a gear as if for a gradient
no one can see, and I've pulled over

at a sudden plastering of hail,
the windscreen blenching, wipers
at a loss – as suddenly

cleared…and up a shaft
of swept sky, on a thermal clean
as a piston, two rise, almost casual,

leaning to the camber of the air (half air
themselves in their feathers and bones),
their wingtips nearly touching, hand-

over-hand-hauled up by double helix
torque, a force that looks for all the world
like ease.

Itch

A sound like blown grit stops him
in the street: that bush, brown-brittle-boned,
all twig still in March, and each twig end
a locked pod. There must be a wind;

he hadn't noticed, hadn't noticed much
since morning. Until now: that sound
that says *grasshoppers*... or the itch
of the *idea* of grasshoppers in his mind

filtered in from somewhere else, as tinny
motel ventilation ducts bring tiny
voices in, like cats bring mice. That day,

that field, that summer: everybody his age
had one once. Where's his, with whom and when?
That damned noise. *Scratch, scratch* goes his pen.

Seedfall

Tipping over the hedge, a flounce like down-
dust from a plumped-up duvet...

Worlds. The shade of the summerhouse lawn
gives them pause. Like a spatter of snowflakes

on clear water, not sure when or if to melt,
they hesitate. Then pelt together

on a sidestream. Now stop, as if baulked.
There are shapes in the air I can't see.

And voices. Two small girls appear,
intent and central, as if they'd been told

into being by the story that the older leads
the younger into. It tells them away.

Inside the summerhouse's open door
we're unseen as the dark in the eye,

as still as perfect possibility.
A gust. Another seedfall,

flakes of laughter from the party
we've deserted, and one stray

speck hangs, a visible hiatus,
on the threshold then,

as if deciding, comes on in.

Out of Town

Why have we stopped? – her small voice
as the engine coughs. Coughs out.
The tick of metal cooling

like a ratchet being tightened.
And there's the blanket of glow
his headlights try to smooth for her

across the forest floor, and the bare
trunks it singles out, only
to double the shadows between.

Why have we stopped here?
I want to go home. Home
is the rust stain on the sky,

a corrosion of daylight;
home, a penny dropped
behind the skirting of trees,

not to be found again. Pull back
to see now, as an owl's low glide
would see: behind its spilled light,

the Fiesta and him in it, hands
tight on the wheel. He's reduced
to his own silhouette, and her voice

in his head. He's marooned
in the tale, in the night, like the Man
or the Hare In The Moon.

after *The Orange Glow Of Town* by Andrew Cranston

Still Falling
(for R)

What you saw, what you made of that
    moment, I don't know. Maybe
        you'd turned away
    straining on, as a five-year-old should,
        through the nothing-much fête,
        the windy precinct,
    but I glanced back, as a sneak gust took
        the pink and yellow jelly
        of the Bouncy Castle:

a play-earthquake. Then a guy rope snapped
    and the world slipped its moorings.
        lifting slowly. Bright
shell-suited happy-shrieking children, high
    on breaking rules with gravity,
        changed pitch
    as they knew there were no rules at all. *Not*
    my child. Not mine. Touching you
        just to be sure

I steered us away, as if we could leave them
    still and always falling,
        the paving slabs
    waiting for them, and the crowd half turning,
    half not. You don't remember?
        Were you there at all
or have I inked you in, trying to grasp
    how a moment of nothing
        more solid than air,

can be the edge we stumble over, as real
        and not-there as an isobar,
            a system moving in,
        the fingerprint of harm: a sharp word
            in the playground, sharper
                silence in the family,
            and this young life or that or yours can wheel
                out of their parents' reach,
                out of their own,

and we can't call it back, no matter how we tell it?

Lachrymans

Outed from under (the floorboard came up
with a squeal of rusty brads): the smell

like a suspicion passed around the neighbourhood,

just a catch in your throat but sweetish too,
and the spidery forest, mycelium glade

decked out with dust like dewdrops,

and we're on our hands and knees, angling
with a torch and broken mirror – nasty children

spying on a murder in the doll's house.

Just think, all this time, beneath our feet
and shag pile carpets: these secret compartments,

unlit subways sprayed with oxides, rots,

florescent salts, and back there in the dark,
the fruiting body, like a relic in its niche

miraculously weeping: *Merulius lachrymans.*

Floating World

A cut stump rots, look. Look, its edges fray
like rope. A clutch of mushrooms, brown
as what we might compare them to, plumps on decay.
The sunken garden... Then, a pouring sound

overhead, like a sluice gate: eucalyptus leaves
rushing nowhere, like time, always now
and passing. Nightshade, moss, banana trees
float on the surface of themselves. We're drowned.

Werk des Gesichts is getan,
tue nun Herz-Werk... *

* The work of seeing is done.
Now, the work of the heart...

RAINER MARIA RILKE,
'Turning Point'

Chalk Form, with Erosion

Heart of chalk: a particular darkness,
white grain against grain, that leaves
    no room for light.
        Sleep of chalk,

sleep that comes for a lost thing
crouched against a blizzard when the soft
    unending boom
        ends

having filled up the world with its white.
This ground-down shell-scurf, in its micro-
    millions, snows
        out of time

out of mind. (This is for all those
whom forgetfulness has taken. I could name
    names that their owners
        can't recall.)

Mind of chalk: a kind of memory
this happened   and   this   this this
    this   impartial
        as forgetting

and as blank, the open secret whole
cliffs give up daily to wind, rain
    and sea: their white
        is instability,

an always-and-at-any-moment
letting go. And yet just at the point
    of crumbling there's
        this, in-

dividual, upright as Job: this
one, arrived at by subtraction,
    almost as if meant,
        like something

you could put a name to, like
    a kind of self, a
        you, a me

Next to Nothing

...a wasp, a wasp husk, there behind the washstand
in a place he notices whenever he can't reach –
from the bath, or the loo. It will nag him, a little, as
    slightly in fact as that slight

sound there beside him, a bodiless rasping, some
September afternoon: there was a wasp, maybe this one,
scraping pale tracks down a fence post. He found the nest
    in the attic, a papery brain,

and now there's this – grey, desiccated to a crouch
as if trying to stand on almost nothing. He'll sweep it up
later, he thinks. And doesn't. Or does and forgets – it's such
    a next-to-nothing thing –

until who knows when the thought might strike him,
in the long slide of a car crash, or in some consultant's
waiting-room? *Did I?* Its slightness is too much
    to grasp. Like the spot on the sky

where his father showed him Venus, in broad daylight,
not half a wink of brightness brighter but, if you know
where to train your binoculars, there, you see it's never
    not been there.

The Long Walkers

They're coming, I saw them, where a straight
track widened from the burnt horizon,
coming tall and bluish in the sinking light.
The pale coppery edge of sky behind them

ate into their outlines. Hard to guess
the distance as they walked and walked and were
no nearer. They had the stilt-walking grace
of giraffe or okapi, and brought hunger

like a gift, long shaved heads carried steady
as pitchers of water, like the king and queen
of smoke, his hips loose-slung, hers sturdy

as the late light melted him to her to deep-
eyed children of uncertain number, seen
then not seen, coming even as we sleep.

A Prospect of Goole

A flock of blue gantries is suddenly there
  in the flatland, like wading birds
   drawn down the wind

from the north. They all face one way, calm
  as hieroglyphics, with foreknowledge
   of an estuary

so far denied me. Sea into fields, sky seen
  through girders, trade routes
   into heartland, inter-

penetrations everywhere – miles between me
  and Drax, whose cloud-capped
   cooling towers

forge endlessly inland, steam unravelling
  east and away behind them,
   like this train

that feels emptier stop by stop, filling
  with distance, that I vanish in
   whichever way

I turn. I could be getting somewhere.

The Old Order

A strict lawn, cruelly striped. The ark-
archaic sneer of butler rooks. Step in a trans-
figured hush, the heart stilled, fountains
tinkling like a clavichord. Then let us dance.

Excuse the plastic sacks of Blood and Bone.
Urbane and glandular, each fatted rose
has particular tastes, exquisite. *Humour us*,
they say. Only Yorick the gardener really knows.

Mosquito Music

Bare boards, dust-sheeted
shadows... In the corner,
swagged and tented muslin
like mosquito nets

on a foundered four-poster
with one broken upright,
three askew –
a berg that sways and glows

from inside, patchily
with candle flicker.
It could go up
in a scurry of flame,

a pungent sizzle,
daddy-long-leg wings,
this gas-mantle brittleness,
husk and cavity

becoming dangerously brilliant
as streetlights click
precisely out at one a.m.
The cage is draped for sleep

but the canary won't stop singing
in their skin, those two
shapes you might make out
or remember   toss and twist

and tangle; the mosquito
won't stop fizzing, tingling
in some inward crease or fold
        they can't quite reach.

Scenes from the Never Movies

like the one where, *that* scene, are you listening, you remember...?
Where he nudges the silvery E-type, so Sixties, right to the edge
of the pool and, all the party frozen as he takes her by the hand,
opens the door like the gentleman he isn't, clicks their seat belts
(and when did you ever see that in the movies?) Drives off.
Splash. Bubbles rising. Then, big as a bolster, the last gloop
of air. The husband staring, a champagne flute still unspilled...

Or the one where it's a card game. Grim-faced, no one moving
at the table. We notice their tumblers, nearly empty, then
next time we look, half full. Then more, as if time
was spooling backwards...as in cocked-up continuity
or the instant when the universe, expanding, teeters and starts
falling back. The players (anyway, how could they?) never know...

Where the peal of bells rings out – victory, was it,
or a wedding? – and one of them, at full swing, tips
free and we see it tumbling, end over end, the sunlight
making fool's gold of its bronze, as people scatter but
not fast enough. Great Bertram, I think it was called...

Where the Rosicrucian doctor spreads out his map
of the known world. There: the unsuspected continent!
In the time it takes for gentlemen to hold back, hold each other
back, he takes the candle and it shrivels in a rush of flame...

Where the elephants break from the circus, snapping guy ropes,
towing the trawl of the big top down the high street, scooping
comic policemen, tourists, an uncanny little girl... Where two

grim sweepers move aside enough to let the camera through.
Where all possible lives might have been. Where we sat

in the back row, eyes closed. Yes, the one with me, with you.

Her Cake, and Eating It

a glimpse of paradise cuisine
    the lady has bright hungry eyes
a fairy tale of fruit and cream
    and charm school grace and winning ways

crisp darkling bitter chocolate twists
    a glimpse of paradise cuisine
the year's first icing-sugar frost
    a fairytale of fruit and cream

a strawberry flush   a fall of snow
    crisp darkling bitter chocolate twists
behind her smile   a shadow now
    the year's first icing-sugar frost

she wants and wants   she has that look
    a strawberry flush   a fall of snow
she has so much it feels like lack
    behind her smile   a shadow now

November gazing from the eyes of May
    she wants and wants   she has that look
invite her home: *come dine with me*
    she has so much it feels like lack

sometimes she is a stranger to herself
    November gazing from the eyes of May
sometimes Red Riding Hood sometimes the wolf
    invite her home: *come dine with me*

the lady has bright hungry eyes
    sometimes she is a stranger to herself
and charm school grace and winning ways
    sometimes Red Riding Hood sometimes the wolf

Unburglars

When we came down and found the back door open
first it was the dash from room to room – *video?*

stereo? TV? then the private hiding places. All
intact: relief, laced with a rather eager gratitude

like being let off with a caution. Till that night,
tucked down again, every catch and bolt piously

checked, that's when it came in with the calm assurance
of a curse. They *had* been. Come and seen, moved through

the house, hardly stirring the dust on the carpet, taking
it all in. Peeling gloves on like a surgeon's: to them,

a fingerprint would be as gross as skid-marks. And
no need to take a thing – why, when they have it all

and need so little? Little breaths: if they'd bent over you
sleeping (when you could still sleep) how would you know?

Opera Bouffe

The count of cappuccino,
the marquise of meringue,
all the little cantuccini...
and what was the song they sang?

Oh the best of us is nothing
but a sweetening of the air,
a tryst between the teeth and tongue:
we meet and no one's there

though the café's always crowded
as society arrives
and light glints to and fro between
the eyes and rings and knives.

We'll slip away together,
perfect ghosts of appetite,
the balancing of ash on fire
and whim – the mating flight

of amaretti papers,
my *petite montgolfière*,
our lit cage rising weightless
up the lift shaft of the air.

So the count of cappuccino,
the marquise of not much more,
consumed each other's hunger.
Then the crash. And then the war.

Survivors

The message got through, but it was too late:
there was an edge of burning to the sky.
All night by the barges, we were made to wait.

Dark wharf, dark water. More important freight
than us. Some made it, some not. Don't ask why.
The message got through, but it was too late.

Blackout... The city silent. Then the grate
of iron wheels. Grey convoys creeping by.
All night by the barges, we were made to wait.

No time, but time enough to contemplate:
was there a choice? Could someone not comply?
The message got through, but it was too late.

No names. A neighbour? One you used to hate?
Nobody looked each other in the eye.
All night by the barges, we were made to wait.

A lifetime gone, and who's to bear the weight
of proof? You, you were there. And so was I.
All night by the barges, we were made to wait.
The message got through. But it's late, too late.

A Poppy in Black

Peter Reddick, 'Incandescence' (engraving)

                    black poppy
                    nothing
                    nature gives us

                    the dark grail

poppy negative
wind-full
ink spinnaker

bows and bows down

                    and won't break
                    like grandma's old and always
                    maid her treasure

                    she who came and did

little head-in-the-clouds before
the Flanders poppies
bloomed into *that* meaning

sudden as a quarry's drop

                    the cut trench
                    at everyone's feet
                    and still flickering

                    the opposite of flames

on the edge in the wind
like a butterfly's tough
sooty under-wing

with hearts of carbon

seed pods spilling their cup
of knowledge charcoal and
re-squandered light and

us   the work of our hands

taking ink   taking air
taking poppies   the fire
of them   making them

somehow and together   fly

                              *

there and gone between sunset and morning
night poppies
                    nearer to home than you think

the flash-dip of search party torches
that just miss them
                    probing the edge-of-town woods

throw them into relief   see them once
you'll see them anywhere
                    shadows spontaneously grown

a black rag on a stick among the rubble
not surrender
                    but a blind spot in the sniper's aim

so much and no more nature gives us
this grit on the tongue
                    with a dry taste of night

seeds speckling the crust of the bread plait
we break casually
                    not considering it a ritual

the one dot that sticks in your teeth
and punctuates
                    despite you   every smile

Laundry Night

An awe-inspiring cleanliness
took hold of our village of K.
the night of the spring melt starting,

the flood beach of loosening
pebbles alive, with a crackling
sound, like a husk splitting open,

which summoned us out to the pool,
the flat rock where our great-
grandmothers beat their laundry dry.

We were stripping off winter clothes,
down to the buff, and beyond,
but deftly – we'd done this before,

laying out our whole skins and faces
without wrinkles, having drubbed and sudsed
them in the newly-muscled stream.

It is a tender thing, each time,
like a new bloom in its season, our raw
underpinnings stooping gracefully

to rinse and brush our outernesses
clean...shaking them out
in the moonlight like flags of ourselves

then peeling them back on, like surfers
kitted for the new day rising,
ready to return, resume and meet again

(or our children meet their children, our
grandchildren theirs) our good neighbours of J.
who had slain us in our beds the night before.

A God's-Eye-View

What you see is what you get
        best if it's least expected.
                Mountains, I said, *I want*
mountains, as the plane dipped
        out of murk, and there they were
                laid low: Skiddaw, Sca Fell,
Helvellyn... all the grandeur
        of a rucked-up carpet. Then
                we slipped off the edge of the land

over mud in its glory: satin-finish
        steel, streams tooled as fine
                as root-hairs, a rococo river
opening its coils, a pewter plain
        where herds of light grazed,
                prehistoric – on and out to a hem
which was silky then matt, uncertainty
        then sea, for sure. That was a boat.
                The scratch of its wake. But back there,

hadn't that been a shadow,
        stretched by late low sun
                to a many-times-life-size
sign of waving – either at me,
        as if they knew what brilliance
                they were part of, or at a shore
from which they trusted help
        was coming, as the tide turned –
                the figure itself too small to see?

The Life of It

...slips from a spilled
            cloud, a clattering
    trayful, whole canteens
            of forks and knives.
...broods too long
            up its cwm, its grievance
ripening to another thing,
            oh yes and another.
...leaks out of the peat's
            withholdings like grandma's
    preservative tea.
            ...bends to the spit-and-polish
of its raw stone doorsteps.
            ...is tricked down a cleft,
almost interred by bracken,
            draggle-grass and bramble
till it could be the sound
            of moss's moist-and-lushness,
    wood sorrel's dilution
            of dirt-cheap champagne.
    But here, a drop in pitch:
            a sudden inner space
    where practical hydraulics
            spate by drought by spate
    have hollowed swirl-
            pools: systole/diastole,
the sunken current pulses
            till some blockage upstream
shifts and it's the sound
            of every life and likeness,
    white noise in the dark, the song
of gravity, that wants us home, again.

The Quakers of Pompeii

Quaker Meeting (sculpture), Peter Peri

Let's say the ash came down;
    we were forged and preserved.
Here's a good girl, sitting up at table
    waiting to be served.

This woman's big hands
    think nappies, think bleach.
She'll give the world a clip around the earhole
    if it gets within reach.

That man is hugging
    something spiky to his heart.
This one says *Sorry, Sir* (though he's a big
    boy now) *it fell apart*

in my hands. Age
    tenses this one like a spring
or a grasshopper, poised to flick away
    into nothing. Or to sing.

This one's a sit-down striker
    who Will Not Be Moved.
That handcuffed convict waits
    for his appeal to be refused

again, again. This woman stays
    slumped backwards where
somebody knocked her. She hides her face.
    She holds the chair.

The last man frankly
    wants to be excused...
as well we all might if the final flash-
    bulb caught our attitudes,

when the clay we've been moulding
    eventually bakes.
Until then, listen to them breathing. Love
    the fidgets. Love the aches.

Thirty Seconds on the Baltic.

Far out, like fast
dark smoke, now above
the crisp horizon, now below,

it's a tailed kite
with its string cut, twisting
downwind, stretching then gathering...

It veers, to a pure
V of bird purpose, a wide-
harnessed team hauling the wind home,

veers again,
and what to call the moment
when the trickle, never slowing, melts

into part of the grey-
black flicker which is still
the stillness of unbroken Baltic? Life

into things: dare we
say *incarnation* – the everyday
kind, quick, at a slant to us and leaving

no trace except
(where are you now, and
who, as you look up from reading) *this?*

Last Days

And, suddenly, there's no time
      before the vans, the vans
            and then the skip, and then

Completion. Closure: click
      like a changed lock. Beyond which
            here will be somewhere subtly

utterly else, and those dreams
      in which you'll find yourself here
            again, here again, will drift

down someone else's corridors
      like stately-home hauntings
            with their tics and vague tasks

and obsessional routines, half-self-
      forgotten long-stay patients.
            Last to fade is the child

who posted a newspaper page
      just a shred, with the date,
            down a crack in the floorboards,

signed, like his own work...who felt-
      penned his initials on new flesh-
            pink plaster – grave

with the import of it: God
      on the night of the sixth day thinking
            'I could call it *Time*...'

Shell Forms

I

At last
the windings of the inward life
               laid bare –

open house,
every casement, skylight, door
               thrown back and wide,

stripped floor-
boards resonant, and one stray shred
               of curtain lace

making wave-
forms, the visible sound of the sea
               we fancied might reside

here so anyone, even
a child could grasp it, have and hold it
               all – immensity –

in their familiar
grip the way that now they might
               a mobile phone.

II

The open secret:
these folds within folds,
lips and cavities smooth
as mucus or its memory
in rubbed stone, stalagmite
               or ice.

But it's a warm abstraction,
this: everybody's most intimate
intricate spaces. Every
body's. Which makes the distinctions
between us stringent and delicious:
                              nice.

III

At last, let's
  not forget: a soft
    life made this
      to its measure

grain by grain:
  true transcript
    of its growth and harm,
      an exterior soul

abstracted further
  by the tumble-mill
    of surf on shingle,
      purified

for tideline heaven
  among twigs. Claws. Glass
    ground almost semi-precious.
      Polystyrene foam.

The Abstract Garden

I come back more often these days, where I've never been:
    the Almohad garden. The idea of it – cool
        proportions in the formless heat,

a reticence of arches, the pierce-patterning of shade
    like my great-aunt's pepper-shaker. Raised
        paths, sunken ground

kept under leaves, a shared secret, and the pond bed
    dry...with glints, a surface, courtesy
        of last night's spiders.

But the aqueducts are crumbling as we speak;
    the hordes of After have let it all go
        like an unsolved equation,

the court of *al-jibr*, where the known and unknown
    terms converse, the guests of *zero*.
        Imagine it gone,

as good a place to start as any, a ground plan at most
    in the lie of the parking bays out back
        of the new mall. Imagine

yourself, arriving, tourist in another language,
    to be told you're years too late...
        turned away, exhausted

by the flight, by missed connections, misdirections,
    too many faces, camera-flash, screens,
        windscreens and oh,

the longing to peel off the film-thin veneer
    of your self from yourself and

        so

    it occurs, one moment, that
sufficiency of light through screens, of unseen

    paths in combinations
masterful as chess or Go, so simple
you could spend a lifetime in them – ways we might walk,

    even at this late
date, peaceably, alongside anyone,
with not a common word between us. No, closer than that.

The Channel

I'd thought that distance was a kind of cipher,
    nothing in it – an idea the world
had had, that left us on opposite sides of
    an equation. Our first week apart

I found myself doodling its symbol: brackets
    inside-outed. Trust a man
        to translate sadness into mathematics

) (

or ink on the page – like opening a *river*
    of type, so space might flow
between our tight-packed print, for
    clarity, the better to be read:

say *parting* only as in *of-the-Red-*
    Sea (bulging in about to burst,
        a waterfall withheld, above your head).

) (

I'd thought it could be thought, and thought
    away. And then I saw it – miles
of mud and mud-light and mud-water
    widening to sky of much the same:

the estuary. Distance itself. The silhouette
    of a sudden bare island (claimed
        by which side's country, I forget).

) (

A *body of water*, flexing. And the Grounds
    that grow back each tide, each time
changed – mud-marches where nobody stands
    but birds, a conference of them: news

from the tundra. Hush-crackling, with the noise
    auroras make, they peel off. Hiss
        of worm casts. Bird prints in the ooze

) (

already losing definition, like *either* and *or*
    dissolving, where the sea brings tankers
and Atlantic glass eels; each opposite shore
    brings rivers, runoffs, silt and scrap.

I'll meet you there, to claim a land
    that isn't, with our symbol. Let it mean
        not distance, but a kind of *and*.

Tree Form: Baobab

A song
     that sings
         itself

deep taproot
     on a parched rise
         nearly sand

dry leather bag
     of a baobab
         hollow at the heart

containing what
     if we could only
         if we could
             if we

                Too much, too many wavelengths overhead

                    like unravelling wool
               notes unstrung from their staves

                 a speckling interfurling cloud

                     like city starlings
                      like a page

           of newsprint released to the wild

                or locusts   dry clickety
                 megabytes of them

       small hungers that   by being fed   increase

and leave us
in the stripped grove
that was silence

when we still
could hear it
so the art

now is listening
cheek to hard bark
for the one

true rustle
like a thrill   a
just about to thrill

of cymbals
signs of song
that
(if we could only)
themselves

sing

Translated

Coming home after years in Japan
he was a strange guest. *Abstracted*
    was the word they used

as he looked at, yet beyond, the new-
planted box hedge, the fantastically
    exacting roses,

even the Knot Garden, disentangled now
from history – they had thought that,
    at least, might please

but he gazed like one bereft. *Fusoki-
shugi*, he sighed once. A lost
    lover, they guessed,

not knowing the word for Incomplete-
ness, what's left out, that rigorous
    prepared-for grace:

the pool that wasn't, the point where a stream
effaced itself in white quartz sand,
    the plenitude of Less.

One Thing

What is it, made of too much
and too many? It involves it all:
    the dull glows of goldfish leaning up
    to the air chewing gobstopper bubbles,
fuchsia blossoms floating like ditched sailboards

angling in towards the capsized
fountain, its glitter that happens
    to break on a stone, the improbable
    pause before the drops – scarcely visible
pimplings were it not that through the fuchsia twigs

the flaking underbranches are acrawl
with soft ripplings upwards... It involves
    time, the angle of afternoon sun
    so the traffic of light goes slowly on
and on and nowhere up the peeling whitewash wall

and the way it implicates the shadows
of the fuchsia leaves, and so on, endless,
    to no end. Made of many and much,
    it holds us, holds us now like one
thing. Now. The one thing we can't touch.

Still Life with Commas

(after Terry Whybrow)

The room is empty, but
for this: the composure
of two self-sufficient

things – a vase as rounded
as a fruit; an apple
like the fact of gravity –

contained, containing
volumes of which they
will not for the present
speak

    ,

     while we
just by beholding grow
to be part of the space

that holds them, that
they hold – inside their skins
an emptiness, substantial

as the weight of water
on which boats and we,
our breathing bodies,
float

    ,

     a moment
like a place you come to
tilting towards sleep,

a dream that's lucid
in that they, the objects,
are aware of you,

your thirst, your hunger. Here
they level with you. Here
they do, and do not,
care

,

        are there
and not there. They are
neither vase nor apple

but the silence of them
re-composed. In no
house, on no table. Ours

for the taking, I say,
as if such no-things could be
in my, or anybody's,
gift

,

        still life
and in abundance,
limitless because contained

in itself, in its earth
tints, in its holding true
to face us, in its own time,

in its cool and upper room,
its holding of its breath
and yours and mine.

0

And sometimes what I want to say
is

yes, that pause – it's a *yes*
of a pause, like now: I've woken early

just as the bird that's been up sharpening its one note
stops, as the half-grind-half-sigh

of a train across the valley, that I didn't hear
when it was there, becomes its absence,

with everything stepping back to clear a space
in which the day will be erected when the first

shift clocks on. Now, though: a pause...
or many pauses, leaning all together (I sit up

still sleep-warm, in the altogether)
at one point: a point of balance I can't hold

but for a moment here between the tip
of my mapping-pen (0.5mm) and the blank

page, and before the first mark (too much
like a full stop, or the pinprick leak

through which the world will start
to seep, then flood in)

here it is. It isn't nothing. This
is the eye of the needle, and the perfectly

smooth egg of Zero
from which a whole world of number was born.

Jizz

I took it for a smear,
a condensation wraith, side-lit, with cloud behind.
It would not be wiped –

outside the double glazing, out of reach. Rain
came and went. The wisp
restated itself, precisely, that day, and the next,

the next. I took it for a sign.

*

A monoprint, in feather-oil,
not so much of the...pigeon, was it? as of flight
– that moment, the up-tilted

tips of the wings, the camber of its swerve,
the first flare of alarm,
the cross-hatching of breast feathers, intimate;

close up, three dots of blood...

*

A death mask? Or a life
cross-sectioned, clinically, at the point
just before it was not,

before the feathers in the yard, the lice
abandoning the cooling fluff?
Or the jizz of the thing, its just-is, cursive,

unforgeable: a signing off?

*

Firstborn, she writhed
and grizzled, three months old. The struggle.
　　Too much, it was too much,

this *being*. We nearly agreed but, *Poor chick...*
　　Her Cornish great-aunt, she
knew something: *Not enough oil on her feathers.*

　　Sunlight catches it. This is the stuff.

　　　　　　*

That razorbill we salvaged
at the tideline as the oil slick slopped in
　　wave by wave and clung:

wrapped in our picnic blanket, it slashed
　　at us in panic as we soaped
and scrubbed it...then could only watch

　　it die, from too much oil or none.

　　　　　　*

It's our choice: see the sign
as omen: *Leave this house, go.* Or as a thing
　　of beauty (certainly a thing,

though almost without mass, a trace of grease
　　that twists some stray light
to a gesture like a blessing. Spread wings.)

　　Either way, we are addressed.

　　　　　　*

It could have been days
ago. *Crack.* We've been living, without knowing,
    in the afterlife of it

as we do daily with the almosts: just a shade
    more contrast, a reflection,
the Passover mark on the lintel...and a small

    death sees and veers away.

                *

    Surface tension. (Glass
is a liquid, though slower than most.) Us,
    we were nothing to it,

swooping at a wide and clear (reflected) sky.
    I sat and began to write
this in a service station with (believe me)

    Greatest Soul Hits Ever
in the background. *I hear you knocking*, goes
    the chorus, *but you can't come in.*